About the Author

He's a lovely man. He lives in Devon now. He's done a lot of things, like keep bees, design buildings and landscapes for sacred use, build the buildings too, have kids, lecture in fine art, watch birds endlessly, farm a smallholding, live in Osho's communes and in cities and in desert places on several continents, teach art as therapy, make furniture, write articles for international magazines, do nothing in a cave, exhibit his paintings, grow organic vegetables, have lots of grandchildren, write a book and get really into beekeeping.

These poems are the work of the last three years, the drawings of the last thirty.

Life is one Blessed *thing after another*

rashid maxwell

Published by Tree Tongue
2 Chapel Downs Cottages,
Crediton, Devon. EX17 3PB
www.treetongue.co.uk

ISBN 0-9546099-2-1

Offering

Poems are a form of concentrated protein
nuts nourish and they store the future tree

please feel free to relish them
eat them and excrete them

in the bio-physics of this planet
everything bears fruit

these protean poems of my heart I offer to
beloved Nisheetha
my children and their children
and to all the Lovers

You will know who you are!

Contents

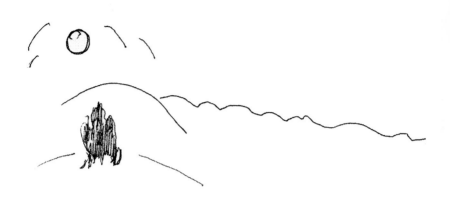

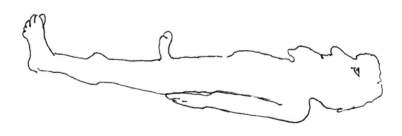

Where Do Poems Come From?

if
you
want
to know
how short poems
are born come now with me
stop listen wait till you hear the clean
sound of nothing see jackdaws beat their ancient
pathways in the air above the garden or find the badger's
long-established trail across the patient wood throughout
the afternoon work with single-mindedness hoeing the
beds picking up corms, seeds and roots of poems
later with your handy garden trowel plant
them out carefully in warm light well
drained soil wherever you might
happen to be then you let
nature take its course
whatever it might
happen to
be

October

the high blue sky is empty of the rushing loops of swallows
the oak leaves are as green as meadows and the meadows are the colour
    of a desert
summer has undoubtedly departed
now rooks and jackdaws wallow in the underwater currents of my breast

both my daughters called me yesterday in tears
these days it's not so often that they get to see each other what with
    children
husbands household cares I left their mother after many years when they
    were little
they called to tell me of the love they feel abounding

October is the month of equilibrium
Nature ripens and decays in balance
I tell myself a story of a world where seasons are suspended
in balmy air where birdsong is perpetual

the cherry trees and lime trees bow to the unpreventable
the red gold clutch of autumn.
I stopped the car outside a churchyard with its ancient rebel yew
and elegant tower

in the north transept I caught the flash of mediaeval glass -
colours pristine like the morning after illness -
at my feet were three unusual brasses
rooks and jackdaws rode the underwater currents of my breast

My stepdaughter called later and I told her of the glass and brasses
she remembered forty years ago we cycled through the lanes of Suffolk
visiting churches with brass rubbing graphite and rolls of paper
I never did that with my daughters

love is a breaking up of boundaries – this and that no longer separate –
living in the story
that we tell ourselves we miss the world where colours glow and seasons
are suspended

which is exactly this world here
exactly this world here

Looking Back

looking back
it seems
this life began
when my master smiled at me
twenty seven years ago
tomorrow

the former life lives on
brilliant in the branching
sons and daughters
and the scattered
fruit
of destiny

do you remember
the blue skies the luminous
red flowers of the ashram
always first in line for discourse
worked my ass off in the veggie garden
meditated

learned to fly
a sunken submarine
when he died singing as
the flames consumed his body
awash in tears
of gratitude

now the friends
daring in their trust
are scattered
the dangerous bloom
of lovingness emits
its fragrance

we don't look back as a rule
he's in our every molecule

21 JAN '03

Time

Mondays I put money in the kitty
Tuesday is the meeting at the apiary
Wednesdays the dustbins are put out
Thursday nothing much
Fridays we clean house and recycle glass and cardboard
Saturday draw my pension and do shopping
Sundays nothing.

I cannot call my time uneventful.

Imagine someone carefully parking a car-bomb alongside the target.
They climb out and lock the car door. They walk two hundred metres
and stop, turn and press the remote. Imagine the car burst open
and the low level roar and the flames and the pieces of steel and
plastic and glass flying down the street. Imagine one tiny splinter of
that glass as a planet in one galaxy hurtling out from a cosmic Big
Bang. Imagine we are on that glass planet that set out four and a
half billion years ago. Imagine.

The neighbour's grand-daughter must be five already
she's wearing school uniform today.
I need to clean the car
And pay the milkman.

I once came face to face with a leopard in Brazil. He was up on a
bank ten yards away. We were not threatening each other, just wary.
He was almost invisible in the shade. His eyes were as wide and as
patient as oceans. Before he receded I lived an alternate life.

The sound of a contented hive makes me forgetful of myself.

The Vedas say that time is like a horse with seven reins,
unageing, thousand hoofed, ejaculating seeds
huge and shiny like a black lake in the moonlight.
Our job is to mount him
jump him through the cardboard wall of death.

I cannot call my time eventful either.

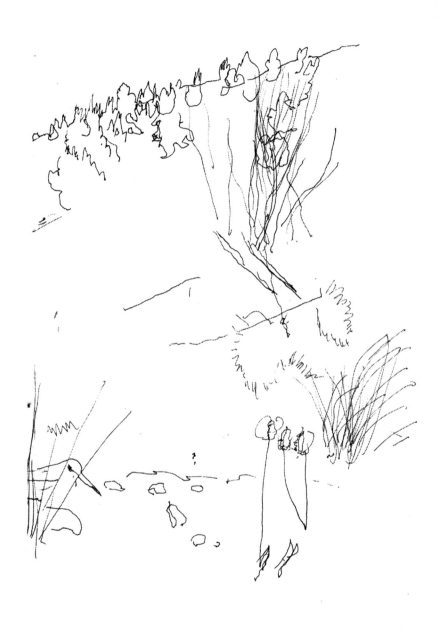

Riddle

In lazy moments after all the sweating and the sweetness

                                            can't be spoken

in the long blue shadows of a summer evening

                                            can't be seen

using brilliant intuitions of the mind

                                    can't be understood

ascending with the flute and violin

                                        can't be heard

on the sleeping child's cheek

                                        can't be felt

never coming
never going
can't be brought or left behind
pointless hopeless unbelievable imbedded

who are you?

Occluded Front

OM

The moment caught me
pinned me
where I stood between
the rows of scarlet runner beans
and the wood of dark oaks
that leans too far across my
garden
with a sudden darkening of the skies
rain fell
torrential rain

the sound was all enveloping
the sound of bliss maybe
all the landscape shapes were bleached
and blurred
each colour shared itself with every other colour
water soaked through to my underwear
a cool embrace
an honour
nature bringing to itself a part of itself

after all
where the beans come from and the rain and the pair of owls
in the dark wood so too do I.

With a basket full of lettuces onions beans and sweet courgettes
I stand beneath a tree and think oh its global warming rain this
rain way too heavy for the time of year in England I see the dark
birds of the multi-nationals tearing every tiny morsel from the
earth's tegument I think the politicians should be weeping on their
knees before the children of the world
war and poverty disease and terror
this must be our future now   where did we go wrong?

Look how we exclude ourselves from everything outside our skin!
look how the rain includes!

H2OM

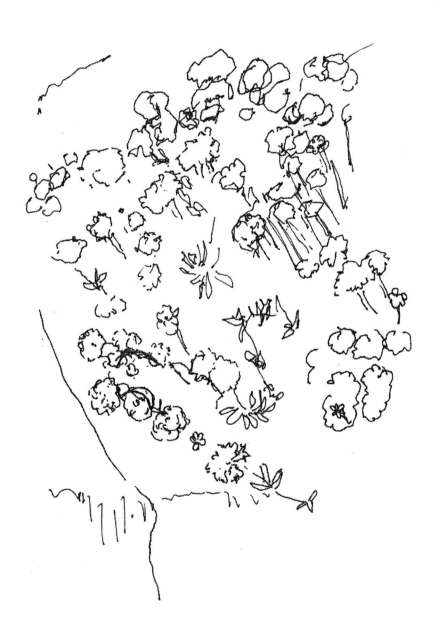

Self Portrait

We artists think we are saying the unsayable. Nothing is in truth
sayable. Talking
about this is missing that. Good work, bad work, it's all the same.
Serenity,
catastrophe are neither here nor there. All real things are forever
poised above the Void; water-boatmen skating on the
surface tension of the mind. If a word so much
as brushes them - BaZap! – they're sucked in.

And it's no good. It's no good
avoiding the void.
We are that.

Void

Is that a Primrose?

This morning
            dropping down
                    through the woods
                                I feel the annual surge
Of life returning

Snowdrops stand immaculate
            across the rufous litter of the leaves
A chaffinch is exhilarating
            high up in a sky-washed oak
The newly-minted air
            teems with spring
                    quickening my feet
                            rising in my legs

I mention this because its been a long damp winter; damp days
seeping into sodden, mildewed observations of our politicians and
priests in purple suede and maggot generals dying of corrupted
spleens while pink, serious men in global corporations set about
accelerating global warming.

                    I think
            What if we lose
        The benevolence of spring?
            What if we lose
        our sense that feels it?

        What if the sunrise goes unnoticed?
            - a glare on the windscreen -
        What if chaffinches are eradicated?
            - disturbers of the peace -
            (warplanes are okay though)
            What if grass is banned?
        - for harbouring destructive vermin -

What I answer is; since when has mankind been in charge anyway?
The fact we do all this to the oceans and the forests and the soil and
the air must be evidence enough that we are not in charge. So then
we are just part of a process – a germ on a tick on a flea on a frog . . .

Is that a primrose?

At Dusk
I saw

xxxxxxxxxxxxxxxxxxxxxxxxxxxxxxxxxxxxxxxxxxxxxxxxxxxxxxxxxxxxx
spread
    randomly   across   the grey-green
darkishness
of   meadow
    a   flock
of lazy   grazing
                  words

xxxxxxxxxxxxxxxxxxxxxxxxxx I xxxxxxxxxxxxxxxxxxxxxxxxxxxxxxxxxxxxxx
climbed up the bank to a gap in the hedge. Maybe they might be
formed into a poem about – oh I don't know – life? art? whether dog
exists? However they must have seen the movement from the
corner of their ever-watchful, communal, big eye,
xxxxxxxxxxxxxxxxxxxxxxxxxxxxxxxxxxxxxxxxxxxxxxxxxxxxxxxxxxxxx
because,
suddenly, they
began a convergent
stampede, pale shapes on
dark, like some ground firework in
spectacular implosion. Typically huddling
incoherent, suffocating. Words don't want
to be picked off, lose their freedom or, as
my son said when he called by chance on
the telephone just as I was writing, "Don't
script them, just know roughly where
you want them to go but not
how you are going
to get them
there."
xxxxxxxxxxxxxxxxxxxxxxxxxxxxxxxxxxxxxxxxxxxxxxxxxxxxxxxxxxxxx
I ducked into the cover of the sunken lane, set off for home. I
aimed my footsteps at the unseen gate just over the hill. In the
twilight I could only see dull tufts of grass on the monochrome of
sloping field. Near the top I stopped and turned;
the
words
were slowly processing
towards me through an open gate
first little phrases punctuation missing
then whole sentences fanning out to create
patterns of beauty, with rhythm and timing and rhyming.

That's how it seems to be - the mind at rest,
everything will work out for the best.

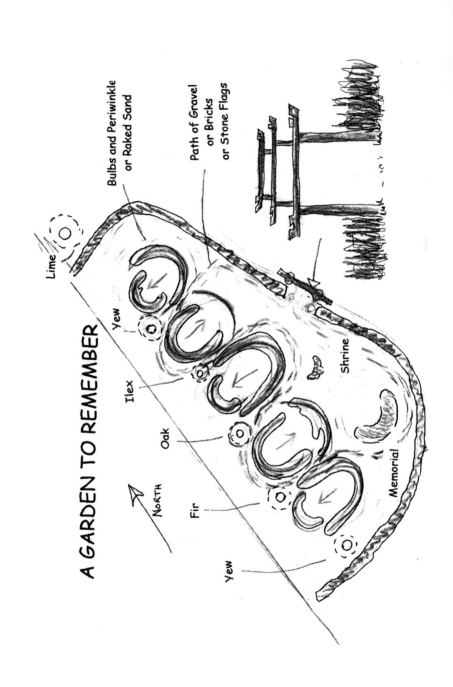

A GARDEN TO REMEMBER

Bulbs and Periwinkle or Raked Sand

Path of Gravel or Bricks or Stone Flags

Lime

Yew

Ilex

Oak

NORTH

Fir

Yew

Shrine

Memorial

A Good Summer

The old canal
gasps
in summer drought

the towpath ambles me
                    towards the long abandoned
                                        two mile
tunnel
through heavy seas of brambles palely flecked with flowers
through faint crescendos of mid-summer insects
through exhalations of small whites and tortoiseshells and ringlets
through the long hot Sundays of my childhood

till i'm stopped beside a lock
thrown down,
asphyxiated these hundred years
by ivy and disuse.

Why now the memory of missiles of depleted uranium fired into Iraq
in a war that we all didn't want and Blair went ahead anyway
because he wants to please Bush claiming that the Iraqi's had great
stockpiles of Weapons of Mass Destruction yet now four months later
in this golden summer nothing has been found and he Blair is saying
history will forgive him anyway if you don't count maimed and
cancered men, women and children as history?

Tall trees stoop over the corpse
of the canal
darkly
the air grows chill
the tunnel mouth slat-gated
exudes
the chill reek
of broken promises.

Of course isn't everything in some sort of balance that we cannot see
without a huge overview yet sometimes glimpse don't good and bad
come back to back aren't death and life standing side by side aren't
politicians just as much part of the whole as the swifts screaming
through their aerial meal invisible above the wood?

The Purple Loosestrife and the Meadowsweet do well this year.
On the way home a shower catches me.

Brilliant Place

Maybe I don't have to leave
this brilliant resting place.

I've been loaded down with too much weight.
'Be somebody!' my dad said.
'Get ahead and stay ahead!'
I was carrying his father's hopes as well.

I got a head; a very, very heavy one.

Maybe I don't have to write a book, or stifle irritation, or fit into the empty slot
because,
this empty slot,
this brilliant resting place
from where all things arise,
is
who I am.

Conversation

If Bush is re-elected – it's
(you want to hear what I think?)
the end of civilization as we know it

Aren't you being a bit extreme?

Finally the whole world in the power of
corporate America; those who wish can wipe out
all dissent
now the bottom line has floated to the top -

If you think such things, how can you go on living?

Life energy that moves in voters is the force that moves
in molecules and hovers in the space
between the molecules
organizes
stripes on zebras and a colony of fifty
thousand bees to pollinate a million flowers – it penetrates
my cranium as melodies
of summer breezes in the tops of trees
builds
into my twin grandchildren their differences
you can even - on occasions - read it in the whirling clear night sky -

*Then does it matter whether Bush is re-elected - whether civilization
as we know it ends?*

Only
if we take existence personally

I Don't Believe in Old

I don't believe in old -
I still can do
as much as ever
these days however
I would rather not

Old is a dirty habit
and I would rather not

I don't believe in old
until I'm sick
then
I am a rusty bollard
on a dock
where no ships come

I long for long unbroken time and I fear the empty days
just let the high seas and the sea mist disassemble me let
water - nature's softest force - corrode my iron core

Old is a breaker's yard
And I would rather not
I'm walking backwards to the bridge
that spans
from here to here

In the shower in the morning
a state of non-existence
flushes out the tyrants of the past and future

old is a dirty habit
that can't survive the present

Meditation Isn't What it Used To Be

Misery has great potential
when the high gate in the prison wall is banged shut –
when lonely hours bleed me stagnant –
when you turn your back on me –
I go into a room and
close the door and close my eyes
the murkiness settles
the clear stream takes me to the ocean.

That was how it used to be. Nowadays when
I close my eyes, I fall asleep.
Meditation is dark matter. It swallows life alive
has presence everywhere
(words scramble from the nozzle of this pen like wasps out of an apple
the hand that holds this pen is old, possibly my father's; the white
sun of late summer and the cadmium blue sky and the still
hedgerows and this scented rose are always, always here.
.... until they're not.)

There used to be misery and a clear stream to carry
my freight of manufactured bliss.
Now there's just the writing and the lighting
and expanding mattering.

Thank You in Anticipation

Thank you for this bright morning
Thank you for calling Cheltenham and Gloucester
Thank you for software, thank you for toasters
Thank you for health hazard warnings.

Thank you for driving with care through our village
Thank you for audiocassettes
Thank you for foxgloves, thank you for fridges
Thank you for glowing sunsets.

Thank you for refraining from smoking
Thank you for kid's sense of humour
Thank you for houses, thank you for string
Thank you for fast-track money transfer.

Thank you for taking the time to cooperate
Thank you for cars with a heater
Thank you for warblers, thank you for mates
Thank you for, more than anything else in the whole wide world,
Nisheetha.

That Stuff

What crossed my mind
As I looked back across the dance floor was
Spindrift. Foam scudding on the surface of the ocean.

I was on my way outside to smoke a cigarette with my daughter in law.
I said, "There's my first ex-wife and her first husband chatting with
her fourth husband and across from them is my second ex-wife with
her third husband and my present partner.
To think of all the shit we went through! Pain and blame and strife
and jealousy and infidelity and law suites. Now look! Twenty years
down the line."

In my mind the dance floor was suspended in the ocean of infinity;
the ocean that sustains us.
The ocean is
Suchness.
Tathagata.
Love.
The ocean is what is and we are wavelets.
All our mighty dramas
Foam,
Spindrift, scudding on the swell.

"Yeah," said my daughter in law, "We have to go through that stuff."

Retrospective

first
we got it together
in a field of wheat

today I hang the painting of you
in my bedroom

she gave me
swimming lessons
in a cornfield
floatation practice
in the silken morning air
what we talked of didn't matter
we were learning how to stay afloat

your face and graceful neck
are painted with a single brush stroke
outlined
by your foxglove jumper and your tree-trunk hair

my wife and I were battered cold war warriors at the time
with combat fatigue and low survival rates
I did not know that feeling guilty was a baited trap

I'm so grateful to you and I see the painting shows it
as you lean into the high-backed chair
away from scarlet cyclamen that press you
like a press-man's microphone

she gave me back
my body and my heart
and
you see
inspiration
burnt umber vermilion and rose madder

that was over thirty years ago
what we talked of doesn't matter
we never saw each other ever after

in a field of wheat.
you gave me back myself

everything in life's an opening
and an opportunity
for thank-you

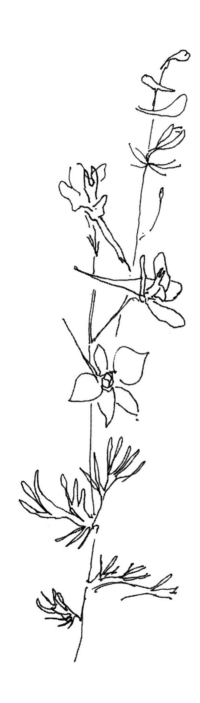

Observing Tendencies
and one indecency

1 raindrops spread across the window pane in even chaos.
2 each raindrop is itself a galaxy of particles.
3 they wait for something else to move them on.
4 sad winter hovers, smothering the exactitude of hedgerows, woods and fields.
5 electrons are not explained by Newtonian or Quantum Physics.

I long for the Spring (at least the daffodils and willows are an omen.)
I long for the Light.

6 the neighbour comes out in her nightgown, arms wrapped round her, waits; her dog spends ninety seconds watering the clematis.
7 no observation.
8 a shiver of the west wind ripples through the dark Leylandii, the naked, inward roses.

Ramesh calls people, 'Vibrating energies'. If we are intelligent and have free will, he asks, why do we produce WMDs? His answer is; Everything just happens. There is no individual doer.

9 on the window-sill there stands a money plant, a succulent from Africa. His branches - formal as a candelabra - are tapering and ringed. His leaves are well-upholstered surfboards.
10 inside his branches there is space for prides of resting leopards.
11 he too is on the lookout for some sun.

Be in the bath but not of it, the bright rounded rows of a verse.
Roses in beauty beloved, embraced in the ground of gold.
Hollow of cradle your morning, yellow and purple your freeing.

12 all this sensory world of raindrops, daffodils and dogs squeeze as light waves through the pupil of my eye and are projected upside down upon my retina.
13 then they trot as waves of wild electrons to my brain.
14 a galaxy of other particles might live there too.
15 no observation.

I stopped my daily meditation. I was a spiritual commuter. There used to be an opening there, now it's sealed with plate glass. I keep looking for the handle.
Are we moved - like raindrops - without cause?

16 a rainbow wraps around my hand.
17 downstairs there is a ferocious dog
18 I walk downstairs. Its dark and I am scared. It's something that I have to risk.

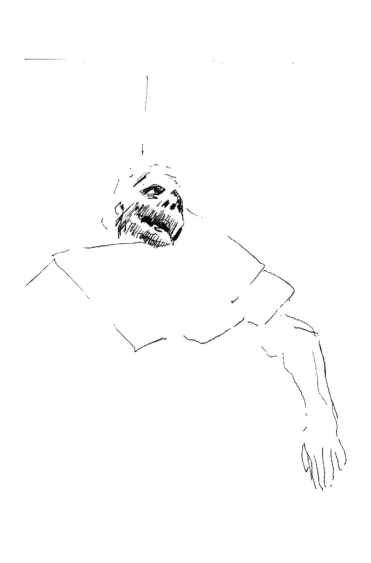

One Day . . .

bedding down the garden for the winter
the spade turns up a dusky corm of what
was till recently a brilliant yellow
star-burst lily

the oak trees have surrendered
their foxy coloured
leaves their rain song is stripped down
to plainsong

winter falls and huge bruised clouds
process into the west
becoming cold I head for
home
light a fire the split oak log
smells of acceptance
is the colour of eastern skin
now when the room is warm that log
shrinks a velvet black
patterned by blooms
of ash

in the charity shop the dry cleaned
suits of unknown people told me
with clarity that one day I will not be wearing
this body

Amazing

Amazing! Would you look at that? A day
of greens and autumn ochres, yellows, reds,
shuffling into dim autumnal grey:
the sky sunk in neglected flower beds.

Amazing! When I take a morning shower,
robbed of thoughts I stand there void - a child;
moments magnify - become an hour
life and death have met as friends and smiled.

This life-long maze! Love deepens into friendliness,
poems happen, bees brew liquid sunset,
I celebrate men's empathy and women's loveliness,
build heart-homes for Iraq and poor Tibet.

Who should I thank for such amazing presents?
No body. Each moment has a Presence.

Buttercups

I eat my whortleberry words along the verges leading to the garden
and the beehives the strimmer tumbles yellow buttercups and purple
sorrel in amongst the tidy stems of grasses those words squat across
the way like anti-tank defences flowers undo themselves so readily
to butterflies to mowers to our covetous delight butter-cupping-
anti-think-tanks that's who I'd like to be like the whole of me
swaying forward to life to the light both saint and sinner thorn and
stamen purpling and yellowing away way beyond all warbled words
I
ask
myself
who am I?
forensic evidence
suggests I am some sort of
pervert a criminal of unsound mind
a creative genius a mister nice guy and an
empty sky all my doings are terminally
irrelevant and whose very being is
eternally seasonable and
infinitely of the
essential
I
we
play
free
from
mine
yours
suffer
willingly
sunshine
hailstones
mower blades
global warming
moths chemical fertiliser
sharp frosts slugs anthrax
(theirs and ours and naturally occurring)
erosion acid rain the feet of badgers man and ants
roundup bumble-bees moonlight bonfires the whole bang existence.

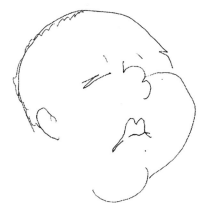

Ciara Audrey Maxwell

Ciara
The dark one
Be the dark one!

Darkness
Has a softness and a depth that reaches
The Beyond

In my arms in Holland Park
Just two days from the moment when you slipped into the world
You were the Infinite

The ineffable
Teeming with every possibility
Every inconceivability

Ciara
Swimming in your parent's adoration, teach us to be
Dark ones

Dolphins
Playing in the ocean's turbulence, eagles on the morning thermals
At home with emptiness

Your face
Is the smallest valley that begets a mountain
Of silence

Ciara
The dark one
Teach us to be dark ones!

Come On!

Where are you when I need you?
You say, 'Here. Always here.'
You say I don't have to look for you,
You say, 'I am you.'

The last blackbird calling at sundown,
the oak tree merging with the sky,
is that who we are?
You don't say anything.

So the silence crisping at the edge of Being,
is that you?
The pulsing at my temples, my breath?
You wink

then look away, pretending
to be a goods train of words
crossing the arid page.
Ok, two can play at that!

I'll wait outside, cook wild mushroom risotto
clear the brambles
write a poem with my back turned,
Come on! Surprise me!

Dream World

Another perfect day in paradox
lost
funeral parties of the raging poor
rush
their battered coffins through the narrow streets
gone
my money passports reasons for visit
gone
I seek sanctuary with the rich and fearful
in their hell
of rundown buildings and corroded hearts.

I'm tired of being lost and tired
tired too of my own predictable company
ready to step out of this
too precious personality

I wake. I hear the primal scream
waking to the dream; not from the dream.

Energy

Energy wells upwards from earth's captivity.
The sweetest plums grow highest on the tree.
A sea of energy bores freely through eternity,
Listen to its hissing thisness. In tranquility
it showers a thousand star-sun's bounty.

These wonders have no form or boundary,
They ripen, burst asunder, they are you - are me

5·31·86

Fog

for Pamela

Fog rolls off the estuary. By noon
the banks of Knot and Curlew lift into the hazy sun.
My spirit soars with them -
everything is perfect as it is.

Feverish in bed - today I missed
the whole point of my life. I'm one of half a dozen billion
rats lost in a maze -
everything is as it should be.

An earthquake; forty thousand die. America
secures it's ownership of mother earth's petroleum
scatters seeds of discord –
everything is just right.

Some have realised who they are. They open
the windows of their long-time home; and from the light within,
the flame leaps to our heart –
everything that is, is fitting.

Death and love and pain and beauty. We steer
amongst the physics of our life and the mystery that we live.
Fog rolls from the hazy sun –
everything is perfect as it is.

Haiku

The C of Consciousness

Bows forward
in awe
becomes a zerO

Flooded with thoughts
I give up meditation
In the hot shower after ahhh!

The sound of barking outside
The dog who was attacked
is a bit bitter

Lorikeets sang along with
Fairy Wrens
What a wedding Joseph had!

High Achiever

What was it I had wanted to achieve
when the tide turns – folding back into itself
and the lone and cockled beach reaches
                                    from sky to sky?
Was it three lines on the back page of the local paper?

What was it I had wanted to achieve
when the rattling train hurries to its next appointment
and the track stretches forever behind the
                                    banks of brambles?
Was it to lose myself in the pink maze of a rose?

What was it I had wanted to achieve
when the overhead grumbling of a 747 tapers away
and the whisper of silence overwhelms the night
                                    on and on?
Was it a party in my honour with speeches and a toast?

What was it I had wanted to achieve
when thoughts recede from the brain
and the body does not know or recognise
                                    who I am?
Wasn't it already achieved, this timeless space and silence?

Hollocombe

Hollocombe this afternoon
is so intensely hot
that nothing stirs

Everything is moving inwards
living its life
the ash tree blurred and bountiful beside the sewage works
a Marbled White
this poppy deeply mottled like an oriental rug
pigeons insects shrilling buzzards

Here's a beetle visiting
sweat pooling in my collarbones shall I plant out the lettuces or wait
until
low pressure brings the rain?

Now he's climbing up my foot
so flat and black
his edge is fraying out to indigo
a prayer mat with a fringe of indigo

The beetroots and the onions and the spinach and the rhubarb
not doing anything
are living life
moving inwards

*Into a Dublin pub comes Paddy Murphy, looking like he'd been run
over by a train. His arm is in a sling, his nose is bloody, his face is
cut and bruised and he's walking with a limp. "What happened to
you? asks Sean, the bar tender. "Jamie O'Connor and me had a
fight," says Paddy. "That little shit, O'Connor," says Sean. "He
couldn't do that to you with his fists, he must have had something in
his hand." "That he did," says Paddy, "a shovel is what he had, and a
terrible beating he gave me with it." "Well," says Sean, "you should
have defended yourself, didn't you have something in your hand?"
"That I did," said Paddy. "Mrs. O'Connor's breast, and a thing of
beauty it was, but useless in a fight."*

What poetry!

Everything is moving inwards
horseshoes clopping on the valley lane
the willows have already grown six foot this year
vetches hard-heads thistles brambles
making lists is also
living life
moving inwards

Home and Away

For two appointments late,
     taking corners far too tight,
worrying about the clients,
     i don't enjoy the journey and my driving isn't right.

Returning to the present,
     resting in this instrument of steel,
immediately! the layered greens of summer,
     the rushing woods, the serpentine of road unreel.

Now! Now i'm in the sounding bell
     of now; a hollow column
reaching from below the lowest hell
     to high above the highest heaven.

Unseen pillars do not make a poem-
the sounding bell is soundless - just a coming home.

Hullo-There!

Hullo-there!
Can't you see me?

I'm here. Not just when you are sending words
like lighted candles down the rivers of the world
I'm here when you are dully mowing your suburban lawn
Or sitting watching trains of thought at dawn -
waiting
with impatience
for me -
my rainbows
and unbounded love.

I'm here. But you don't stop to recognize
me, sitting in your seat, seeing through your eyes
you stomp off self-importantly - we could be having fun
I follow like dark matter waiting recollection -
waiting
patiently
for you -
with rainbows
and unconditional love.

Remembering the future will remind
you I am the you you always knew you'd find
a small boy running through a field of flowers
ordinary, spacious and infused with power -
waiting
without waiting
for the love
of being the
waiting.

Hullo . . .

Letter to The Times

Dear Sir

In order to understand what terrorism is,
first we need to understand despair.

Most people in this country, in Europe and the world oppose the Iraq
war. We disbelieved the reasons given by our leaders and foresaw
the hornet's nest result. We see that politicians do not listen to our
views, or consider our Arab neighbours or the world that our children
will inherit.
Why don't they heed us? Free-market democracy and a globalised
economy are tools too clumsy for the well-being of this planet. They
abuse nature, enslave the many and concentrate colossal power into
the hands of a few.

In these times so many miracles occur
for those
who cannot see the great miracle.

The human animal now dominates this finely balanced eco-planet.
Humans can play music and god and havoc with the environment,
the fool and lethal games, they play at kicking balls around a field
and on the fears of others of their species.

Did you hear the rain play in the night
an anthem on the oak leaves and the car roof?
This morning do you see the branches and the wind at play?

The human animal now dominates this finely balanced eco-planet.
Wherever there is trouble in this world – famine war disease
destruction – there is the miracle of man. Can readers of the times
make any sense of all the different problems and all the different
cures and all the contradictory opinions? There is too much
information on the table. That's why we go hungry.

Its not a question of belief.
There is nothing to believe.

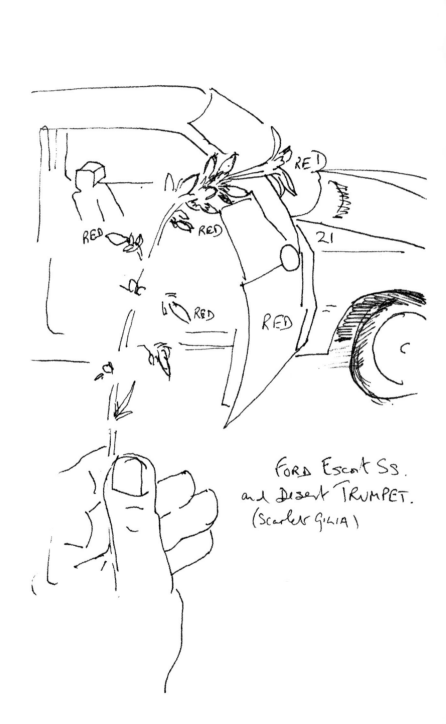

RED

RED

RED

21

RED

RED

RED

FORD Escort SS.
and Desert TRUMPET.
(Scarlet GILIA)

The human being's mind, his miraculous, demonic mind is just a servant who has taken over while the master is away. He hands us out our passports and our credit cards, gives us politics, religions and the military. The master is the heart. Now is the time to leave the ruined institutions of the mind, walk out beneath the open sky with all its storms and stars.

There is only seeing: seeing clearly.
Change what you can
the rest is miracle

Yours Truly,
rashid Maxwell
Member of the League of Human Beings
4 Shute Wood
Hollocombe
Devon Ex187QJ

23 10 04

Ah ha
I'm a zen monk
Brushing my hair in a sacred city.

like a dog i am . . .

like a dog i am
standing in a windy landscape,
the one who owns me gone.

for years i traveled on the tops of busses,
overheard the women chatter.
the next poem would be the one;
accurate and beautiful.

i sip the light within the trees
swim the viscous spaces
in between the trees
bow down to the rook overhead.

i painted in words
the ribbon of nature
and the song that is not heard
and questioned why raindrops are evenly spaced.

sometimes i
almost understand
these things point to the mystery
and not to whatever i name it.

like a dog i am who waits
for the piercing to the heart whistle
and the steep descent through heather
to the car.

Like Antarctica

We sat on folding canvas chairs
round the fire whose quaking
flames engaged
our eyes and melted down the voices

the night was dark
a false sky
rose from the damp meadows engulfing
the dome tents
she said
it's like Antarctica

we rose and hugged I may be gone
some time he said and in the whispered
song of raindrops on his tent

vanished

Long Winter, Itchy Feet

"Is that the sound of silence that I hear?"
"Shush! Listen silently."
"Is that the ocean I can hear?"
Listen silently."

Winter is a frayed tarpaulin laid across the fallen hills.
I bicker with the wife, fall prone to travel ads, resent
the optimism of the rooks. Spring is doubtless
on its way. Please hurry. I am dying.

"Is that the circulation of the blood I hear?"
"Shush! Listen silently."

Happiness is being where you are.
Unhappiness is wanting to be elsewhere.

*   *   *

Driving into Taunton you pass a grassy area
with cedars, firs and evergreen oaks.
There are no fences, walls or hedges –
a life without boundaries.

"Is that the sound of mental chatter that I hear?"
"Shush! Listen silently."

Much later on I realise that
it is the Taunton cemetery.

*   *   *

Two electrons fired in opposite directions
behave identically even if a million miles apart
Nothing can travel faster than the speed of light.
So how do they communicate?

"Is that the whisper of the cosmic wind?"
"Listen silently."

My body is made up of an ocean of electrons.
I want to know who runs this show I call my Self.

*   *   *

*   *   *

Spring hints sometimes of its brilliant bounty.
I rub my eyes and go back to sleep.
Apple blossom buds now stand like nipples,
time frays; brilliant sunlight mends a tattered meadow.

.

"Is that the sound of one hand clapping?"
"Shush! Listen silently."

Happiness is being where you are.
I am at home, roaring to be elsewhere.

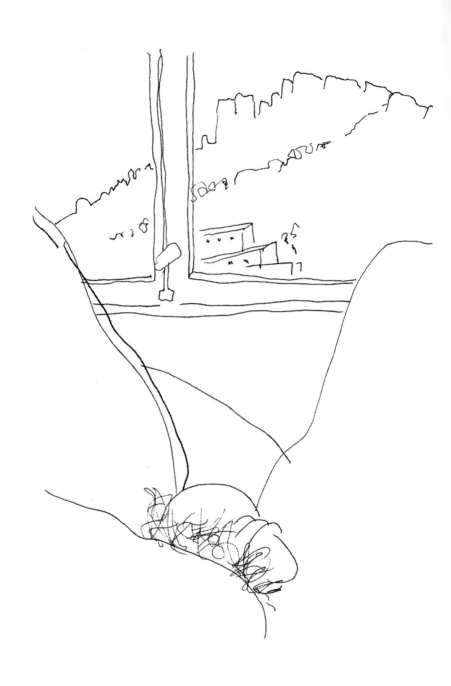

No Body

All afternoon we sweated
planting trees
crab-apple rowan spindle ilex
until dusk
First it was a slight sore throat
then difficulty swallowing
by midnight I was dead.

The life of bodymind is circumscribed in time
like old farm buildings or computer hardware.
I hadn't missed the symptoms
for some years now I'd worn my father's hands
stood singing in strange places to no body
failed to recognised that stiff-backed some body
on closed circuit TV
as me.

I was he who stared at things;
blue-green curving walls of waves,
women,
the birth of my son,
a grey-green winter sky.

Coral builds up on its own detritus
I played in sandpits, planted trees, loved kids and women,
built book-cases and meditation halls,
wrote poems, did the washing-up.

When the use–by date expires,
a consequential nobody (a cosmic Health Inspector)
stands in the whitewashed stable
the animals long gone.
He too sings softly
to no body

Predictive Love SMS

bevoled nod! Some-
werhe benhid the sparlke
me your eeys – smoewerhe
whitin the elegnace me yuor
lnog sirkt, smoewerhe udenr
the wekinrels me yuor sikn
bevoled nod yuor rael
buetay waits to be
kindeld
pealse
anne hree bedsie me
close yuor eeys revome
the sirkt so it wnot ceasre
revome idaes and cares
sit hree arstide me so I
can take a reading me
yuor bueaty with
my sipecal too!

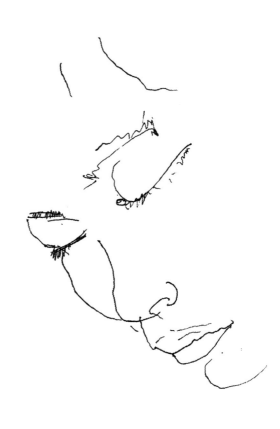

So Fed Up

I am so fed up with waiting
for the cloud to blot me out
fed up that I missed you earlier
in the flavour of wild strawberries
the pattern on the moth's wing

all my life I've waited for the dark one
waiting at the wrong bus stop
I am so fed up

aren't you fed up with me
insisting that I am a writer or a father?
I know I know - you've everything else to do
be light waves and wild strawberries

I am a hunter luring rabbits
calling out the one word - carrot
or a singer singing to call silence up
language is a hammer swinging wildly

Hey! are you breathing through these lungs
writing secret memos through these words
I didn't hear you come
or go

Vision

I see. I see that we create, I see that we sustain, I see that we destroy existences each moment of our lives. I take a thought and from it I write words that no-one understands. It doesn't matter.

There is no future now. This vision goes so deep the thinking mind cannot conceive. There is no time. Worlds and universes separate each moment. There is no past. We create each moment worlds apart. Moment. Moment. Moment. So beautiful.

Big I creates, Big I sustains, Big I allows to tumble into void. The formless is god and thank god I can underwrite this. Creating, maintaining . . . what?

Look!   These buddha drawings and this photo of a Master, the banded bookcase and the ringing telephone, this present line of lower-case camels strolling across the desert page.

Nothing matters because nothing is real. Creating and destroying happens every moment. Reality can change at every moment. This is the truth. The Truth.

The Truth is.

The whole world is created in a flash, a line of camels in the desert, one step, one step, a line across the page, separated by a thousand universes and a small lake in the sky.

Do you see?

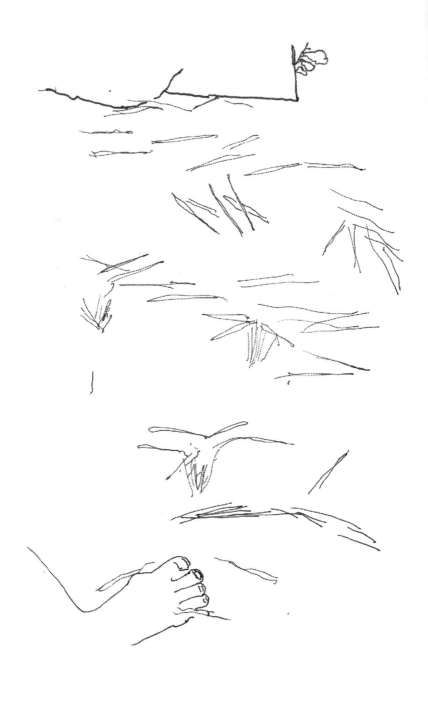

The Stones Need Thanks
For Rajyo before surgery

I wanted to thank them
the round grey stones with white quartz veins

They lean in tiers towards the raking waves
settled into each other
like warrior brothers
letting themselves be worn to sand

They're patient too when human desire enters
hauled to garden centres
called to simulate a stream
become a doorstop or
foundation for a shed
waiting while I fidget
with my digital single lens reflex camera
– I used to love these hands
now they're lumpy and red
I look at them with scorn –

what does it mean
to lean towards the waves that wear them to sand,
to long to be worn to sand?
anyone with a body should thank them

The Art of Dying

The art of living is to learn the art of dying.
Say your head weighs less than half an ounce
inside are women weeping, leaping salmon, and yes,
galaxies that fold forever
into themselves.

Living is a dying
we skate on less than half an inch of ice across
the superconductive, unseen bridge
that keeps us from the sea of death
until it doesn't.

Only death is certain in this life.
everything may be or may not be
when word of death is stuttered down the telephone
or spattered on the pavement then
we understand that only death is certain. Isn't it?

Living is the art of dying
now and now
the heart is always in the present, luscious as a park in summer
while ideas browse like undernourished cattle
out beyond the boundaries.

Living is another word for opening the heart's doors and windows
death could come soon; a passenger jet through your office window
or it could come late; everything in order, pain in the old bones,
turning to the heavens in your son's arms,
I don't want this any more.

Either way, death is the guest who won't be turned away
Who might as well be welcomed
Then everything weighs less than half an ounce and
Everything is welcome.
Isn't it?

The Bridge at Eggesford

Below the bridge at Eggesford
the water from the waterfall
wells up
and spreads
into itself

Like in the early morning
when you're sitting in the bed
and night-time silence
spreads
into your inner self

Inspiration leaps
like salmon
returning
from
an unknown realm

The First Great Western London-bound express bores
through time and space
while salmon leap and
rashid's being spreads
into itself.

The Valley of Clear Air

Anyone
desiring Peace or Love or Inspiration
must burn here like a log - burning in the embers of their live
desires –
reduce their fuel to the ashes of
their Discord, Hate and Dullness.

We saw the valley of clear air; orange groves, a citadel
with infinite rooms and women singing coded mantras;
Dover Wight Plymouth South-westerly gale force eight
High pressure. Variable. Losing its identity.
Good.

The women spread a garden
for humanity to lie in
isn't that why men have nipples?
why we watch the firelight flicker - ancient vision from afar -
and gather strange blooms
of peace and love and inspiration
from the ashes of our own extinction?

The crimson embers flicker in our head,
The valley with clear air is almost certainly the heart.

The Watcher
(For Jessica)

What is your secret dear girl?
How do you know what you know?
Where did you find the flawless pearl
That shines through your Being so?

If you get that life is a play,
And you are the audience of it,
Actor, producer, director, costumier,
Then your life will be lived at a profit.

What do you reckon sweet Jessie
When you watch the Television?
Do you find the lives of celebrities messy?
Can you spare them your derision?

What in the movie is true?
The light on the screen? Or the story?
Is it we in our tiny minds who imbue
The light with the gore and the glory?

We build up the world in our mind
And then we interpret the scene,
It is good or it's bad, it's cruel or it's kind
It means what we want it to mean.

On the pavement you suddenly see
A snake. You jump clear - you hope!
Then you see it again and immediately
You realise it's only a rope.

We endlessly chase a mirage
In the endless desert of mind
We somehow think it is us in charge,
That too is illusion, we find.

Come with me and stand in a wood
And see what happens inside
The voice of the trees can be understood
And they never, ever, lied.

Like a lamp in a windless place
Our mind becomes quiet and still
Then we can see our original face;
The Watcher who waits on the hill.

*   *   *

Transmission

O
one
word
appears
– a muddy leaf along the muddy track –
the reader, Robin,
– plodding upwards through the autumn flurries –
reads the language of the woods

Bajere baje domoro baje,
Nachere nache choruno nache

Live transmission
issues only from vast
silence

O kaninganing go
lai lai o kaninganing go

The leaves – the wor ds – pass out beyond
the limits of our sen ses back into the void
behind our senses for a moment who?

for a moment without time
he is this
emptiness

O

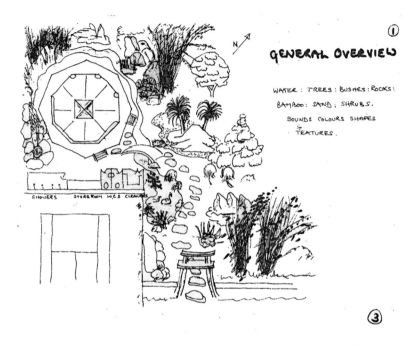

GENERAL OVERVIEW

WATER : TREES : BUSHES : ROCKS :
BAMBOO : SAND : SHRUBS.
SOUNDS COLOURS SHAPES
+ TEXTURES.

SHOWERS   STORE ROOM W.C.S CLEANERS

FLOOR PLAN

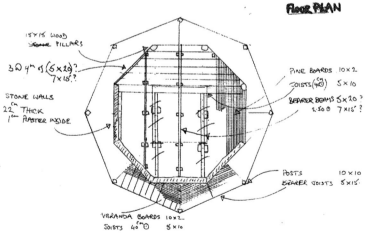

15 × 15 WOOD
~~STONE~~ PILLARS

3 @ 4ᵐ ∅ (5 × 20)?
7 × 15"?

STONE WALLS
22 ᶜᵐ THICK
1 ᶜᵐ PLASTER INSIDE

PINE BOARDS 10 × 2
JOISTS (40ᶜᵐ)   5 × 10
BEARER BEAMS 5 × 20 ?
2.50 @ 7 × 15"?

POSTS   10 × 10
BEARER JOISTS 5 × 15"

VERANDA BOARDS 10 × 2
JOISTS 40 ᶜᵐ ∅   5 × 10

Usual Attitudes

"The man of peace is creative. He is not against war, because to be against anything is to be at war." Osho

Our Baghdad correspondent
visits casualties
of yesterday's precision bombing raid.
That crying five year old - is all of us.
Permanently crippled.

Drifting in the pre-dawn silence
I can not find
my usual attitudes to war.
For or against.
Breath in. Breath out.

And later, feverish,
immersed in streams of
sweat and bulletins,
I'm not myself again.
Mind and body warring.

War.
Small word for suffering:
- recurrent as stones
in the stony desert -
winners and losers
permanently suffering.

Destruction, decay
make humus, the seed bed.
We will suffer or we will
surrender for a new
humane humanity.

The siren wails for all of us
except
the one who seeks
and cannot find
their usual attitudes.

What Walks these Legs?

In the dusk
These legs keep moving
The grey road curves ahead
The colours long since fled
What walks these legs? The countryside is hushed.

More of me is automated
Than is conscious
Heart thumping
Lungs pumping
Mind running like the cistern when the toilet has been flushed.

At home I'll light the fire
The mind will run more slowly
There'll be diversions
Sprawling conversations
Someone has to change a light bulb in the sitting room.

Mind whirring before the event
I nearly missed
The day's last golden splash
Behind that copse of oak and ash
My legs keep wading through the gloom.

Then up the wooden hill to bedfordshire
Clean my teeth
Subside into the deep
Dreamless sleep.
Now where's the walker of my legs?

When I've walked and sat and ate and worried for my kids
Another twenty years, these automated body parts will cease
The silence looking through my eyes
The silence of the empty skies
Won't have to walk these aching legs.

I Could Never

Let's say you are wandering life
trying to establish some sort of link.
Then you encounter an Osho. You stop - you think
YES! But I could never,
never be like him.

Later on you meet unique Ramesh.
Your little ego says that even if I lived a thousand
Hindu lives I'd need another thousand long
long lives to
sing his song.

Then you meet a Gangaji.
You think, she's almost one of us.
Yet even if I was as beautiful as she
is - I still
could never be like her.

Then you meet an Ekhart Tolle.
Not beautiful but totally engaging.
If you too had his skill with words –
to think you'd ever be like him
would be presumptuous folly

Then truth-teller Pamela wafts along
Alight in an ordinary, everyday way.
Witty and pretty and loving and strong
you suddenly start to think perhaps
I too could sing this song.

Silent Thunder

the central heating wakes me sets about its early morning business
humming softly to itself shall i do a sitting meditation now or later?
it is dark i rise and draw the curtains back letting in the silence

yesterday my daughter told me of a pair of school friends who were
staying on the island of Phi Phi in Thailand they went as usual to the
beech that morning he said I'll get my surfboard you wait here later
he stood looking at the waves he said let's go from here they
packed their bags travellers cheques and passport climbed twenty
minutes up a hill at the top they turned and saw the wall of water
tragedy is always punctual

outside dawn peeks gales knock the stuffing from a fleeting crowd of
blue-grey rose-flushed clouds four jackdaws in precision glissade
down the sky pas de chat then plier dans les trees

sometimes in the early morning meditation inklings of eternity arise
the primal void then i go to clean my teeth and make a cup of tea
the telephone intrudes good morning mister rashid maxwell cathy
here from c & g we got your application in the mail this morning you
forgot your passbook silly me!
and bingo! single-handedly i've made the world forget about six days
this takes six seconds

i should be meditating now for a moment there is winter sunshine
pale as weathered straw resting on a counterpane of beech and oak
leaves underneath the scarlet-dotted holly somehow lighting hazel
brushwood from within glowing fire-sticks up against the purple clouds

the bbc world service said the great wave crashed through twenty
miles of jungle the rescuers found bodies everywhere yet not one
animal not a rat nor a snake nor a boar nor an elephant
last night by chance I read about research in 1986 recording calls of
whales and elephants they use a long wave note that carries many
miles but is three octaves lower than the lowest note a human hears
she calls it silent thunder it is visceral not cerebral the frequency
below the calls of birds and animals just above the sound of
earthquakes and large ocean waves my italics

check email sangham of world fellow travellers again the telephone
submerges me draws me into bindweed paradise my daughter's on
her way brew a root soup when will i have time for sitting
meditation? silly me!
meditation is the celebration of what is happening right now.

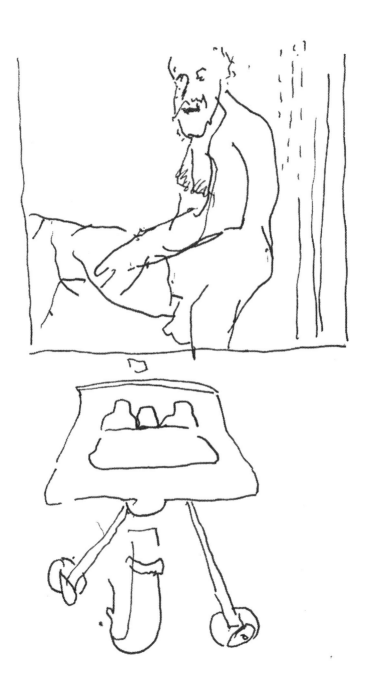

Reflection

The old man's shoulders
droop
his frail frayed hairs
show
the friction of the years. "Is there anything we can
do?"
I ask him.
"Is there some discipline or
practice
for attaining truth?"

"Truth? he echoes. I think he
thinks,
how can anyone
attain
what they already
are?

"I know I know I know all that," I
say.
"Aren't we also human beings; not merely human
doings?"

In a dream last night, the waiter reported me to a passing policeman
for not ordering a dessert. We were in a foreign country. I stormed
out to the police station to clear up this ridiculous misunderstanding.
They made me wrap a tape measure six times round my fist. The
reading off the tape in millimetres was the score of penalty points
against me in some future prosecution. I could choose to pay a fixed
fine then and there and have the slate wiped clean. The waiter and
the police split the proceeds.
I think the dream was telling me existence is a-causal. Truth is not
arrived at by amassing points for good behaviour.

"Doings?" he reiterates. I
guess
he's calling me a doer, poking fun at me because i
need
a practice just to
see
what's obvious right in front of me - that
this image is a mirage.

With that reflection he turns away
as I do from the mirror.

Arunachala One

On Shiva's fiery phallus
an avalanche of sun and rock
has all but stemmed the ooze
of thought and word that makes me
who I am.

Up here the sage Ramana
lost his self and found impersonal Self,
became I AM
in this blind cave beneath the bodhi and the mango trees
where monkeys bounce and bicker.

Who am I?
The word of god, I hear, is silence,
all the rest is peacock cries

Arunachala Two

Like a plane whose pilot
wants to taxi everywhere
I write these verses out of
unexamined, existential fear.

At dawn we fuel up
there in Bhagwan Ramana's cave
we think that we have lift off but
you can't steal silence from a mountain.

We could free-fall of course
freedom is our hidden face
I met a laughing Buddha
she said trust your guru's grace -

stay in that consuming sun
where guru, god and you are one

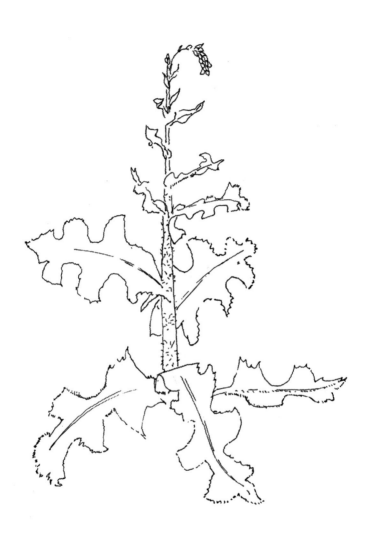

Arunachala Three

'That's how you know sannyasins,' said the girl. 'Osho's
people are so right there: present.'
I was following Pradakshina, the pilgrim path around
Shiva's mountain Arunachala in South India.
Remembering the words, I clean forgot that I was here
on holy ground.
The mind is such a monkey!

I kept walking, seeing silverbill finches
iridescent butterflies, one green - one turquoise
termite trails on sapling teak trees
strings of dried up limes beside the way
the Shiva symbol painted as way markers on the rocks
and stones, a lingam of two white strokes and one
rufous
red faced macaques grooming in the shade of
eucalyptus trees
the dusty rusty tired volcanic earth
signs of cattle grazing in a freshly planted forest nursery
human faeces (naturally)
a kingfisher.

This small journey had the colourful potential of a poem.
I started sketching it out in my head.

Thus I lost my way.

Osho
thank you for the gift of love
and for my name
for the wisdom in your teachings
for ears to hear the secret song
for eyes to see what is not visible
for the gift of meditation
for these tears that purge my heart
for sharpening our intelligence
for kundalini meditation
and for the sangham of your lovers
of whom I am most blessed to be one
thank you

Printed in the United Kingdom
by Lightning Source UK Ltd.
122317UK00001B/104/A